Self Confidence Secrets

Self Confidence Secrets

Quickly and Easily Boost Your Self Esteem and Confidence Today so You Can Start to Achieve Anything, Make More Money, and Live the Life You've Always Wanted

Chuck Rikard

Softpress Publishing

Copyright © 2014 Softpress Publishing

All rights reserved.

No part of this publication may be reproduced, distributed, or transmitted in any form or by any means, electronic or mechanical, including photocopying and recording, or by any information storage and retrieval system, without the prior written permission of the publisher, except in the case of brief quotations embodied in critical reviews and certain other non-commercial uses permitted by copyright law.

SOFTPRESS PUBLISHING
4118 Hickory Crossroads Road
Kenly, NC 27542
www.softpresspublishing.com

ISBN-10: 1-4995-2092-1
ISBN-13: 978-1-4995-2092-7

Disclaimer:
The advice and strategies contained herein may not be suitable for every situation. This work is sold with the understanding that the publisher is not engaged in rendering medical or other professional advice or services. The publisher does not specifically endorse any company or product mentioned or cited in this document. Websites listed were accurate at the time of publishing but may have changed or disappeared between when it was written and when it is read.

No responsibility or liability is assumed by the publisher for any injury, damage or financial loss sustained to persons of property from the use of this information, personal or otherwise, either directly or indirectly. While every effort has been made to ensure reliability and accuracy of the information within, all liability, negligence or otherwise, from any use, misuse or abuse of the operation of any methods, strategies, instructions or ideas contained in the material herein, is sole responsibility of the reader.

All information is generalized, presented for informational purposes only and presented "as is" without warranty or guarantee of any kind.

All trademarks and brands referred to in this book are for illustrative purposes only, are the property of their respective owners and not affiliated with this publication in any way.

Table of Contents

Introduction ix
Chapter 1 - Importance of Self-Confidence 1
   Understanding Your Self-Confidence Level 3
Chapter 2 - Identifying Insecurities 6
   Exercise 1 8
Chapter 3 - Effective Management of Insecurities 10
   Positive Thinking 12
   Exercise 2 13
   Quieting Your Mind 14
Chapter 4 - Failure is Your Friend 17
   Exercise 3 18
Chapter 5 - Overcoming Shyness 21
   The Three Main Traits of Shyness: 22
   Shucking the Shyness Label 23
   Exercise 4 24
   Starting a Conversation 24
Chapter 6 - Achieving Your Goals 27
   Exercise 5 29
   Work in Your Strengths 31
Chapter 7 - Health and Wellbeing 35
   Establish Principles 37
Chapter 8 - 10+1 Quick Confidence Boosters 40
Conclusion 44

Introduction

I want to thank you and congratulate you for purchasing my book, "Self Confidence Secrets: Quickly and Easily Boost Your Self Esteem and Confidence Today so You Can Start to Achieve Anything, Make More Money, and Live the Life You've Always Wanted".

This book contains proven steps and strategies on how to increase your self-confidence quickly to give you the best chance possible at living a happy, full life and achieving all your goals and dreams.

I have included many techniques and exercises to assist you with learning how to change your life for the better and boost your self-esteem. Using these tools will bolster your confidence today and give you a lifetime full of meaning and happiness.

Thanks again for purchasing this book, I hope you enjoy it!

Chapter 1 - Importance of Self-Confidence

"Unfortunately, unless we're focused on building up our courage, which gives us our self-confidence and all that we need to make quantum change in our lives, the voice of fear will always take the lead inside our minds."
~Debbie Ford

Self-confidence is something we all need, but unfortunately, we can't just run out to the store and buy it. It is something that must come from within and for some, it can be incredibly difficult to achieve. This book is going to help you boost your self-confidence, which in turn will help you lead a more fulfilled life and achieve your goals and dreams.

If you are reading this book, you are probably feeling a little down on yourself. You may not even know why you don't love yourself as much as you should. Somebody who has low self-esteem will likely show it in a variety of ways and unfortunately, those ways are not always healthy.

You deserve to be happy and you deserve to love yourself, you just need a little help finding the qualities that prove you are worthy. We are going to take your hand and lead you on a path that will boost your self-esteem and give you the confidence you need to take on the world.

SELF-CONFIDENCE SECRETS

Let's talk about what self-confidence is.

By definition self-confidence means: *realistic trust or belief in one's own judgment, abilities, and powers.*

Self-esteem is similar: *a realistic respect for or favorable impression of oneself.*

Your level of confidence directly affects your self-esteem and a lower self-confidence translates to a lower self-esteem. As you can see self-esteem and self-confidence go hand in hand and will be used interchangeably throughout this text.

If you are lacking in self-confidence, you likely second guess yourself or are afraid to try something new because you don't think you can. You feel inferior to others as if you are not as good or as deserving as those around you. You are worried you don't have the ability to complete a task as it should be done. You likely feel as if you have no power over what happens to you at work, home or school.

Another key indicator of somebody who feels poorly about themselves is their relationships with others. It is very common for somebody with a low level of self-confidence to get stuck in unhealthy relationships that deplete what is left of their self-esteem. These relationships are dangerous and will negatively impact a person's life. These relationships can be with parents, co-workers and romantic interests to name a few. Without a healthy self-confidence, it is nearly impossible to have a meaningful, loving relationship with anybody. You have probably heard it before, "you have to love yourself in order for others to love you."

IMPORTANCE OF SELF-CONFIDENCE

Self-confidence is important to have in the work place, in your social circles and in your home life. When you are lacking in confidence, you will hold yourself back. You are your own worst enemy. This is not the way you want to be any longer. **You want to be your own best friend!**

You have the power within you to do anything you set your mind to and we are going to show you how. Self-confidence is a powerful tool. You just need to learn how to find it, build it up and use it!

If your feelings were not enough to convince you to start working on your self-confidence level, how about a little scientific proof? A study[1] published a couple of years ago proved that people who had a lot of self-confidence were more successful than those who had little confidence, but more talent. The study also indicates that those with a strong self-confidence level were listened to more by their peers and bosses and ultimately had a huge impact on decisions that were made. Confident people tend to achieve higher social and professional statuses than those who are lacking.

You deserve the status, pay raise and whatever else is associated with your ability to do your job well and achieve your goals. Don't let opportunities pass you by because you are afraid to speak up.

Understanding Your Self-Confidence Level

You may be wondering how your current level of self-confidence came to be. There are numerous factors that affect this. While it isn't right to blame our parents for every little problem we suffer from today, self-confidence is usually something we begin to develop when we are around the age of two or three. Subsequently, our parents play a huge role in our current level of self-confidence. Children who are reassured of their value and worth will often grow up with a healthy self-esteem.

Kids whose parents tend to be extremely critical and are quick to point out shortcomings or perceived failures are more likely to struggle with self-confidence. Now, this isn't the time to blame your parents and be angry with them. However, if you do have kids, this bit of information should definitely be an eye opener for you.

As you age social groups can also play a role in your self-confidence. In fact, before you rush to judgment on your parents, you should know that in some cases, peers are more influential than parents. There is a reason wise men advise you to choose your friends judiciously. Kids tend to be a little mean from time to time. If you didn't have parents at home who were bolstering your self-esteem and then you found yourself in a peer group that was equally lacking in support, your self-confidence never got the chance to bloom.

As adults, it is easier to identify toxic relationships, but it is not always easy to decide what to do, especially if your self-confidence has been trampled. You have to have the confidence to tell a friend he isn't healthy for you to be around. If he can't support you or encourage you, he does not need to be in your inner circle. The reality is, as you start down the road of building up your self-confidence, you may be forced to do a little friend-cleansing. Don't worry about being alone, because later in the book we are going to discuss how to make new friends that like you for who you are.

IMPORTANCE OF SELF-CONFIDENCE

The following chapters will help you identify signs your self-confidence is being damaged. After getting rid of the bad influences in your life it will be time to take the necessary steps to free yourself of all the unhelpful and unwanted negative feelings. If you are ready to get started on boosting your self-esteem today, read on!

Chapter 2 - Identifying Insecurities

"I think thinking about becoming an adult, and having to face up to your problems and face up to your insecurities, is difficult for everybody."
~Mary Elizabeth Winstead

This part is extremely important, but it may make you feel a little uncomfortable at first. This is completely normal! Think of it as looking under the hood of a car to diagnose a problem. We need to take a little peek inside your head to see what is holding you back from being a confident person. You may have heard the phrase that the first step to recovery is identifying and admitting you have a problem. Therefore, the first step to building up your self-confidence will be to identify what is knocking your confidence down.

Don't be ashamed of your insecurities and imperfections. *Nobody* is perfect. Imagine how boring the world would be if everybody was the same and everybody was perfect. Mistakes and trials are what make us who we are and give us our individuality. Be proud of what you *have* accomplished and refuse to dwell on the little things that were not as successful as you had hoped.

Before we get started identifying your insecurities, it is important to point out what insecurity is.

IDENTIFYING INSECURITIES

Insecurity: *lack of confidence; self-doubt; precarious; vulnerable.*

Most likely, you may not even realize the decisions you make are due to a lack of confidence. You will probably not be able to immediately recognize certain actions and choices in your life have been made because of various insecurities that were developed from your childhood. As you grow, so do your insecurities. They take deeper root within your personality and become a part of you. They are parasites and you don't need them!

The following is a list of signs of someone whose confidence level is low:

- Making decisions based on what other people say or do;
- Avoid taking risks for fear of failure;
- Use negative self-talk or diminishing your successes;
- Regularly talking about how great you are at certain things;
- Hiding mistakes for fear of being looked down on;
- Ignore compliments or denying you are worthy of praise;
- Bullying or manipulating other people;
- Allow others to make decisions for you and then complain about it;
- Often feel doubt;

- Hoarding or collecting materialistic things
- Extremely jealous of others
- Promiscuity
- Addictions to dangerous habits;
- Violence;
- Extreme shyness.

You may exhibit just a couple of these signs or several. While it seems there are some conflicting signs, like bullying and shyness, everybody exhibits their insecurities in their own way. Frequently a person will become a bully for fear of letting others see their weaknesses. Violence is a similar behavior. A person must exert their physical strength over others to prove he is powerful because inside he doesn't truly feel that way.

Insecurity looks different on each person. You may have other signs that are not listed. The list is certainly not all-inclusive. If you can identify with even one or two items on this list, you will definitely benefit from reading the remainder of this book and utilizing the included tips and exercises.

Exercise 1

Utilizing a pen and paper or notecard, write out the traits you identify with from the list above. You may want to include other traits that aren't given. **Don't be too hard on yourself** but do be honest and really think about how you act and how others may perceive you.

IDENTIFYING INSECURITIES

Do you make the decisions in your relationship and refuse to compromise? Or, do you allow your other half to make all of the decisions but silently grumble about the poor decision?

Do you have routines that are safe and comfortable and leave you afraid to try something new like wearing a different color or visiting a new club with friends?

After you have your own list, go back and look at it carefully. Can you change anything on that list? Yes, you can! In the next chapter, we are going to discuss how to manage those insecurities.

Chapter 3 - Effective Management of Insecurities

> *"I discovered that my insecurities and my flaws were things that I actually need to embrace, and I let them become my superpowers."*
> ~Skylar Grey

Now that you have identified your insecurities, it is time to decide how you are going to manage them. There is always a solution, but some insecurities will need to be handled differently than others. Part of the learning to be more self-confident process includes understanding why you feel a certain way and how you can overcome or manage those feelings.

Not all insecurities are necessarily a negative thing. In fact, it can be humbling when we are a little unsure of ourselves. The trick is finding the right balance. We don't want our insecurities to disable us, but we don't want to be so confident we fail because we assume we cannot. People who are over confident have just as many troubles as those who are lacking.

There are some signs you will want to recognize that indicate an insecurity is creeping up on you. Identifying these signs will help you manage your apprehensiveness. The goal is to deal with those feelings and not simply cope with them. Coping basically means you have to suffer through something that

EFFECTIVE MANAGEMENT OF INSECURITIES

makes you uncomfortable. That is not the goal at all and will only serve to injure your self-confidence in the long run. Repressing those feelings will hinder you over and over until you work them out and figure out how to manage them.

Some insecurities that are not necessarily bad are those that reveal you are a little nervous, but you are still going to do whatever it is that is making your heartbeat faster. You can compare the feelings to your first time riding a roller coaster or flying in an airplane. You feel a little apprehensive at first, but ultimately, you do it and realize it was a lot of fun and it made you feel exhilarated.

A lot of our insecurities can be chalked up to mind over matter. We get ourselves all worked up and it is all for naught. Our minds are very powerful, and we can turn the slightest detail into a major catastrophe. Here are some of the physical signs you are letting insecurities creep up on you.

- Elevated heart rate;
- Excessive sweating;
- Sweaty palms;
- Upset stomach;
- Irritability.

These are very common signs of apprehension. When you start to notice these symptoms, it is time to take control of your overactive brain and begin *managing* the insecurities that are causing these symptoms instead of just coping with them. Next up we will cover some of the quickest, easiest ways to manage the symptoms effectively.

Positive Thinking

Positive thinking is the quickest way to stop most insecurities dead in their tracks. You are your own best cheerleader and with your positive words of encouragement, you can manage your insecurities. There are hundreds of quotes from wise people like Abraham Lincoln, Norman Vincent Peale, and Alphonse Karr about the power of positive thinking. It is a practice that has been used for hundreds of years for a reason—it works! Some of the most successful people in the world, Henry Ford for example, have expressed how important failure was to their massive success. Without it, they would have never been able to achieve the great things they did. They persevered and so can you.

> *"Failure is simply the opportunity to begin again, this time more intelligently."*
> ~Henry Ford

So, what is positive thinking? Basically, it is you having a little conversation with yourself. Typically, this is done silently, unless you are alone in your car or maybe in your bedroom or bathroom. You would give yourself a little pep talk pointing out the positive aspects of a certain situation. Below are some things you could say or think in a positive thinking situation.

- I *can* do this.

- This may be tough, but I *will* get through it.

- I *can* learn to do this.

EFFECTIVE MANAGEMENT OF INSECURITIES

- The first time may be difficult, but I *can* learn.

- There is a better way and I *will* find it.

- I *will* do this today, so I am not worried about it tomorrow.

- One step at a time and I *will* get this done.

Substitute the word 'this' for whatever task or situation is at hand. Sometimes you need to say these positive affirmations over and over until they sink in. That is fine. Make it your personal mantra. Think of that story from your childhood about the Little Engine That Could. "I think I can, I think I can, I KNOW I can."

Positive thinking is about stating a fact instead of relying on the "I hope I can" or the "I will try," kind of statements. It is important you convince yourself that no task is too hard for you.

Exercise 2

Go into your bathroom and face your mirror. Identify 5 things you like about yourself and say them out loud while looking in the mirror. It doesn't only have to be physical characteristics. If you like that you can do math in your head, say it. If you think you have really pretty eyes say it. Positive affirmations will help boost your self-confidence while training your brain to focus on the things you like about yourself, rather than the things you are not quite as comfortable with.

The first couple times you do this it may feel a little awkward and even be tough. Once you start reprogramming your way of thinking, it will become much easier. It is a good idea to do this every morning before you head off to work, school or to the store. Think of it as giving yourself a shot of self-esteem like you would drink a cup of coffee for energy.

Quieting Your Mind

> *"Dedicating some time to meditation is a meaningful expression of caring for yourself that can help you move through the mire of feeling unworthy of recovery. As your mind grows quieter and more spacious, you can begin to see self-defeating thought patterns for what they are, and open up to other, more positive options."*
> ~Sharon Salzberg

Another great tactic you can use to get those insecurities under control is by "shushing" them. When things get wild and out of control, you are likely to put your fingers to your lips and shush the noise. When your brain gets revved up and starts shooting out rapid fire negative messages that feed your insecurities, you have to step in and take control. You need to quiet your mind and allow reason to rein supreme. Insecurities do not have to control your life. You can manage them.

Quieting your mind is a strategy people have been using forever. There are several different ways to do it depending on what you are most comfortable with. Meditation, prayer and exercise are some of the ways you can take your overactive mind down a notch or two.

There are several techniques that yogis use to block out their chaotic surroundings to find inner peace and quiet. However, you don't have to be a yogi to master these methods.

Meditation—this does not mean you sit on the floor cross-legged and chant. Meditation simply means spending a few minutes in a quiet place where you are comfortable. There

EFFECTIVE MANAGEMENT OF INSECURITIES

should be no distractions. This means shutting off your phone, computer screen, television and whatever else may interrupt your complete peace and quiet. Take a few deep breaths and consciously relax every muscle in your body starting at your toes and working your way up to your head.

This is a great exercise to do before you embark on an adventure or other situation that you know will test your ability to manage your insecurities. Dedicate about 10 minutes to mediating prior to facing something that makes you feel apprehensive. In fact, putting aside time every day for meditation is ideal. It is like practicing your jump shot in basketball. When the time comes for you to use meditation in a desperate situation, you want to be good at it. Practicing mediation everyday will make it second nature for you and you won't have to concentrate so hard on relaxing.

Deep Breathing-You can use deep breathing anytime throughout the day. It is especially effective when used in combination with one of the other management techniques listed here. Take several deep breaths in through your nose and exhale slowly through your mouth. Imagine yourself blowing out the tension and apprehension you are feeling as you exhale.

Prayer—if you are a religious person, you can soothe your nerves by taking a few minutes to pray. You may want to pray before you head out for the day or before you undertake a new task. Give yourself the time you need to say a meaningful prayer. As with meditation, you need a few minutes of nothing but peace and quiet to center yourself while talking with your God.

Exercise—this is an effective way to release any tension you have due to the symptoms caused by insecurities. You don't need to go to the gym. Take a short walk outside or do some yoga moves in your office. You need to release the negative energy that is polluting your body. Shake it out and you will feel much better. Give yourself about 10 to 15 minutes to use exercise as a management tool.

Chapter 4 - Failure is Your Friend

"Fear stifles our thinking and actions. It creates indecisiveness that results in stagnation. I have known talented people who procrastinate indefinitely rather than risk failure. Lost opportunities cause erosion of confidence, and the downward spiral begins."
~Charles Stanley

Nobody sets out to fail, but it does happen from time to time. It is a part of life and is not nearly as big a deal as many of us make it out to be. In fact, if we look back at the majority of our mistakes, we can usually see a valuable lesson that was learned that we can put to use in future decisions. Failure is your friend. Despite the negative connotation associated with failure, it isn't so bad— the key is to focus on what you learned going through it and not the outcome.

Failure is the cornerstone of each of your insecurities. You are afraid to try something new because you fear you will fail. Fear keeps us in our comfortable, safe zone and refuses to let us out to experience life. You probably heard your mother lecture you a hundred times about trying peas or broccoli. You were adamant you didn't like the vegetables and refused to even give them a taste. She argued you can't like what you haven't tasted.

She was right! How do you know you will fail at something if you never try?

There are several reasons why you want to befriend failure. You have probably already experienced the benefits of failure in your life and may not even know it. Have you ever taken a wrong turn on the way to work or to a friend's house? The wrong turn took you somewhere you didn't want to be. You were frustrated and angry with yourself for making such a mistake. Look beyond the anger and frustration and recognize the bonus of the situation. You will now know not to take that road again. The irritation of the moment will help cement the memory into your brain, so you won't soon forget.

Sometimes failure rocks your world, but you don't have to fear it or dwell on it. Your first step after any failure is to own it. Make it yours and do NOT point fingers in every direction trying to find somebody else to blame for your shortcomings. You will never learn if you cannot accept that maybe, just maybe you are the one responsible for your lack of success in a particular project or experience. Remember, it isn't a bad thing. It means you just got that much wiser.

"I have a lot of insecurities, but you learn from your failures."
~Helmut Lang

The following exercise will help you learn how to make failure a valuable part of your life.

Exercise 3

You need to see failure as a part of your success. This exercise will help you figure out what that looks and feels like. If you have a recent experience to use as an example, use it. Otherwise,

FAILURE IS YOUR FRIEND

the next time you have what you perceive is a failure ask yourself a few pertinent questions:

1. Why didn't I succeed as I had hoped and planned?
2. Were the shortcomings within my control?
3. What can I do differently next time to ensure success?
4. What can I do to prepare myself to make it work next time?
5. What can I learn from this setback?

When you answer each of these questions, you are turning that failure into a learning tool. There really is no better teacher in the world than failure. A favorite quote that may help you succeed is this:

> *"You are only a failure when you quit trying."*
> ~Joyce Meyer

Think of a video game or something similar. How many times do you have to play a level until you move to the next one? Each time you play you are learning something new and are figuring out how to succeed. Failure in life is essentially the same thing. Yes, it stings a bit more when we don't get that job we were hoping for or botch a presentation at work, but it is a learning process.

It is also important for you to consider all the benefits of failure. There truly are many glorious things that happen after you have failed. Unfortunately, you usually don't see the plus side of things because you are so mired in your own self-loathing and despair. Wouldn't it feel good to be able to smile after you just bombed your first attempt at cooking dinner for your special someone? Maybe you could even laugh a bit.

SELF-CONFIDENCE SECRETS

The next time you fail to complete something you set out to do, use some of the methods from the previous chapter to take control of your brain and stop the negative feelings from ruining your after-failure glow. Step back and examine the situation and begin listing all the positives that can be found in your botched attempt. If you need to, write these down on a little piece of paper, a note card or put it on a memo in your phone. Here are a few ideas to help get you started.

- Failure is the secret to finding out what doesn't work.
- Failure builds character and helps shape who I am.
- Failure proves I tried.
- Failure identifies areas that I may have been complacent.
- Failure gives you the chance to start over, with a new intelligence.

Stash the card in your wallet or in a compartment in your purse so when you feel as if you just can't do anything right you can pull it out and re-set your mind on the positive aspects of the situation.

Obviously, you don't start something hoping you will fail, but when it does happen, embrace it. Failure may bring you down, but don't let it define you or keep you down. Otherwise, your failures will feed your insecurities and lower your self-esteem. You can boost your self-confidence by understanding that although something may be dressed up as a failure, there is a little success in there somewhere. You just have to dig a little deeper to see it.

Chapter 5 - Overcoming Shyness

"A lot of vices that I've had over the years were always to make up for some sort of character deficiency, one of them being shyness."
~Saul Hudson (aka: 'Slash')

One of the most common side effects of low self-esteem or low self-confidence is a tendency to be incredibly shy. People who suffer from a lack of self-confidence often convince themselves that others will automatically see their faults the moment they open their mouths or show their face in a room.

This keeps a shy person from talking to new people or going out to social gatherings for fear of being laid bare for the world to see. It is tough to make new friends, acquaintances or even find a partner to grow old with if you don't meet new people. Extreme shyness can cause a person to feel very real physical and emotional discomfort. All the symptoms of anxiety that were listed in Chapter 3 are typically felt when somebody who is shy is thrust into a social encounter.

Fortunately, you can overcome your shyness and live a full, productive life. Sometimes, we don't want to talk to people because we are afraid they won't like us, or we won't like them. Is there really any harm in discovering you don't mesh well with another person? Let's say you meet someone at your best friend's party and you chat for a few minutes before you discover you and this new person have nothing in common and a friendship is likely not possible. That's totally okay! No harm, no foul. You don't have to be everybody's best friend!

Talking with others who share your opinions and beliefs is rewarding. Talking with those who are your exact opposite can also be rewarding and enlightening. Unfortunately, when a person is hindered by shyness, it prevents them from seeing and hearing all the world has to offer.

Before we talk about getting over shyness, let's talk about what it is and how it affects you mentally and physically.

Shyness: *tending to avoid something because of nervousness, fear, or dislike.*

Are you seeing a trend here? Nearly every symptom a person with low confidence experiences can be blamed directly on a lack of self-esteem.

The Three Main Traits of Shyness:

Negative Self Opinion-Social situations make you hyper-aware of yourself and how you are perceived by others. You feel as if you are not worthy and everybody else is beautiful, smart or talented and you are an interloper.

Obsessed with Shortcomings-You are so busy identifying each of your perceived shortfalls you can't see the good things about yourself.

Negative Self-Talk-You go on a tangent pointing out everything awful about yourself. You start with something simple like you don't think your shoes match your outfit and end up ripping apart your looks or decide you don't have the talent or brains to be in the room with the crowd that is superior to you.

Shyness feels a lot like anxiety. When somebody does approach you, you may find yourself unable to form coherent sentences because the nerves have got your tongue twisted and your brain turned into mush. All of these physical symptoms further convince you of the above traits. You may not be able to speak, but your mind is in overdrive pointing out each of your embarrassing responses to the anxiety it is producing!

Shucking the Shyness Label

Shyness isn't only about having a poor self-esteem. While it probably starts out that way, the condition is fed by a number of different factors. Over the years, you have been dubbed a "shy person" and you have accepted you are shy. You don't even bother breaking out of the mold because that is a label you have owned. This is holding you back.

Have you ever felt really good about yourself because you did something spectacular or you have a new outfit that fits you like a glove and looks great? You are feeling on top of the world and head into a social gathering ready to mingle, but suddenly you remember you are shy. All that confidence goes flying out the window and you are relegated to assuming your position as the wall flower. **Shuck that label and give yourself a new one.** This is the time to apply Positive Thinking. You are the confident person who loves to meet new people. Repeat it over and over until you own it, until you convince your mind you are **NOT** the wallflower. You **ARE** an outgoing individual who loves meeting new people.

SELF-CONFIDENCE SECRETS

Now that you have <u>decided</u> you are not that shy person, let's make it happen. Overcoming shyness is not something that will happen overnight, but you can do a little something each day. First, let's start by doing an exercise.

Exercise 4

Using that same note card from the last exercise, flip it over and write down a few things you really like about yourself. These are some examples to get you started, but yours will likely look different:

- I have a beautiful smile.
- I know a lot about gardening. (Insert something you are very familiar with)
- I am a nice person to be around.
- I can make other people smile.
- I am witty.

Your unique traits are what makes you, you. Nobody wants a carbon copy of your sister, friend or co-worker. Sharing similarities and interests is fine, but your unique personality is what makes you special.

Keep your note card with you until you have reprogrammed your brain to recognize you are all of these things. It can take a while and like the old saying goes, practice makes perfect.

Starting a Conversation

Walking up to a complete stranger and starting up a conversation can make almost anybody's heart race a little. You

OVERCOMING SHYNESS

are probably assuming you have to do all the talking and you are worried you won't have anything to say. This may be what has held you back all of this time. Newsflash! **You don't actually have to do all of the talking.** That isn't how a conversation works. That is you giving a speech. There is no point in worrying about something that isn't the truth.

One of the best ways to start a conversation is by getting the other person to talk. This is an excellent way to learn about that person and it puts the ball in their court until you feel more comfortable talking. Yes, you may need to take that first step, but it is painless. All it involves is you speaking a few sentences and from there, the conversation will start to flow. The pressure is taken off of you and you will be more likely to engage in a real, meaningful exchange.

These are some tips to help get the conversation flowing when meeting a new person. You will want to tweak it for the situation and the person you are approaching.

1. I love your dog! What breed is he?
2. Isn't this a lovely view?
3. I love that purse! Where did you get it?
4. How did you do today at the game?
5. How long have you worked for Mr. Jones?

Once you have asked the question that sets the conversation ball rolling, pay attention to the other person's answers. Relax and let the conversation flow. You will likely identify more prompts in the other person's answers. As the conversation starts to gain speed, you will likely be asked questions. Be prepared to answer in full sentences, not just yes or no responses. This will keep the conversation flowing smoothly.

It is very common for others to join in your conversation as well. Within minutes, you will have already broken the ice with several people and will begin to feel more comfortable in your environment. You will have successfully broken out of that shyness shell you have been wearing forever.

Chapter 6 - Achieving Your Goals

"What you get by achieving your goals is not as important as what you become by achieving your goals."
~Henry David Thoreau

It is no secret that the people in this world who are confident are the ones who tend to achieve the greatest success. It can be extremely difficult to sit back and watch a co-worker get promoted over you when you know you are a better employee. The person who got promoted is outgoing and reached out to the boss and asked for the promotion. Even though you always delivered top notch work, you sat back and did your best to blend in to your surroundings. This is a common scenario, but you can change it.

You are building up that self-confidence, which means you are going to feel comfortable speaking up and letting the boss know you are around and you are a fabulous employee. You are going to be okay with accepting the credit you deserve for all of your hard work. When you walk into the office, you are going to command some attention with your confident stride and posture.

Before we get too far into bolstering your self-esteem, please realize there is a balance between being over-confident and extremely shy. You want to be somewhere right in the middle.

SELF-CONFIDENCE SECRETS

It is okay to acknowledge when you did something great and it is okay to accept the praise you are due. It is annoying and sometimes downright rude to strut around like a peacock telling anybody who will listen how great you are. There is a word for that—arrogant. Arrogant means you have crossed the line and need to pull back a bit. Arrogance will not win you any friends and will ultimately cost you a few along with any respect you have earned.

Being confident in yourself is a requirement for success. You will not be able to achieve your goals if you don't start developing some self-confidence today. You have to believe you can actually do it before you can ever succeed. Sure, you may have a few doubts when you set a goal to get an 'A' on your term paper or get promoted, but ultimately, you know you are good enough and you know you *can* do it.

If you lack self-confidence, you will never even try to reach your goals – you probably won't even be able to set any. You will find yourself stuck in a rut and quickly heading into a world of despair over your situation. However, inaction is much worse than trying and failing.

Why do you need a healthy self-confidence to succeed in reaching your goals?

- You will have the courage to try, to start something new and uncertain.

- You will believe in yourself enough to move forward with a goal.

- You will have the desire and drive necessary to succeed.

- You can say no to things you don't like or will waste your time.

- Your confidence will eliminate the fear that holds you back.

- You can say yes when an exciting opportunity is presented instead of fearing the unknown.

- Your confidence allows you to set lofty goals that will help you achieve great results instead of small goals that give you very little success.

- You can tactfully defend yourself and command the respect you deserve with flair.

The following exercise will help you define specific goals that will ultimately boost your self-confidence!

Exercise 5

Get out your pen and paper again and get ready to write down three goals. These goals can be anything you choose, with one requirement—they must be "**smart!**"

So, what are "**smart**" goals? There is a great approach to goal writing someone came up with that is called the "SMART" method:

    S - Specific
    M - Manageable
    A - Achievable/Attainable
    R - Realistic
    T - Timebound

SELF-CONFIDENCE SECRETS

You can use this tool to create short term goals and long term goals. For this exercise, write down one long term and two short term goals. Long term can be anything that takes a year or more to achieve while short term should take anywhere from a few days to several weeks or even months to achieve.

You can choose to make these professional or personal goals. At least one in each would be best. Remember to use the SMART method to evaluate your goals once you have written them down. A goal without a time frame or deadline is simply an idea and not a true goal.

Let's look at a few 'bad' goal examples:

- Pay off a credit card – no time frame makes this a bad goal. Also, it isn't very specific.

- Buy a car – again, no time frame or specifics.

- Get promotion from stock clerk to chief accountant in 6 months – while this one has a timeframe and some specifics it doesn't appear very realistic or achievable.

Now let's look at some examples of <u>good</u> long term goals:

- Pay off my Visa card by December 31st.

- Buy a home within 2 years where the mortgage payment is no more than 25% of my take home pay.

- Get a promotion to regional supervisor by 3rd quarter next year.

- Graduate from college with a 'B' average by spring semester.

ACHIEVING YOUR GOALS

- Learn to speak conversational Spanish within the next 12 months.

Here are some examples of <u>good</u> short term goals:

- Learn how to cook a pot roast for our family gathering next Sunday.

- Organize my closet this weekend.

- Eliminate soda from my diet for the next 30 days.

- Exercise for one hour at least 3 days a week for the next 6 months.

- Finish a painting the rocking chairs on the front porch by the end of the month.

Tailor your goals to things you may have been putting off for a while. Start small and work your way up. As you complete each goal, you will get a healthy dose of self-confidence. There is really nothing more satisfying then checking off a task or goal. It is exhilarating and proves to yourself that you can do things you never thought you would.

Once you get in the habit of writing out your goals, check off each one when you complete it. You may want to even add the date. Keep the completed notecards handy and look back over them periodically. It will give you a boost because you will be able to see how much you have achieved.

Work in Your Strengths

Earlier you wrote down some of your strengths. Now it is time to pull out that list or refer to your memory and put those strengths to work for you. You have probably heard things like, "work on your weaknesses and turn them into strengths." How about something a little different that is more effective? **Maximize your strengths to improve your weaknesses.**

> *"Over the years, I've learned that a confident Person doesn't concentrate or focus on their weaknesses - they maximize their strengths."*
> ~Joyce Meyer

Here's how this works. You cannot be perfect at everything. That is silly and futile and will only stress you out and cause disappointment when you fail to turn a weakness into an amazing strength. Working hard to improve a weakness takes away from valuable time and energy you could be applying to your strengths.

To help explain the point, let's use a football team as an example. Each player has a position they are really good at and that is what they play in a game, so the team has the best chance at winning. Sure, the quarterback could probably play a defensive end, but he likely isn't going to be very good at it. Is there really any point in him working extremely hard to get better at that position? No, because there are others who are naturally good at it and the QB is naturally good at throwing the ball. It is how the team works best.

You can apply the same line of thinking to your home life, professional life or social life. Human nature makes us social creatures. We tend to seek out those who have similar interests but are better at some things than we are. **It works!** Why fix something that works so beautifully if it isn't broken? If you are naturally a good cook, you probably do the cooking at home and in your social circles. Your spouse may be better at balancing

ACHIEVING YOUR GOALS

the budget or your friend may be better at choosing the perfect wine to match your meal. The bottom line is we all have strengths and we all have weaknesses. Cater to your strengths and surround yourself with others who can make up for your weaknesses.

> *"Enter every activity without giving mental recognition to the possibility of defeat. Concentrate on your strengths, instead of your weaknesses... on your powers, instead of your problems."*
> ~Paul J. Meyer

When you are working towards a goal, let's say getting a promotion at work, you will need to outline the steps necessary to get that promotion. You may need to do the following:

- Be on time, if not a little early every day
- Prepare outstanding reports
- Be organized
- Give great presentations
- Impress the boss with your knowledge
- Be committed

However, maybe your lack of self-esteem has given you a bit of a disadvantage when it comes to oral presentations. We will identify this trait as your weakness. You have decent organization skills, but you are very good at preparing reports and the boss has already expressed his happiness with your knowledge. You have a colleague who is an excellent public speaker and another who has mastered organization.

Public speaking isn't for everybody. Fretting over your inability to get in front of a room and talk as if you were talking with your best friend is futile. It is something you may be able to slightly improve on, but if you don't have that inner public speaker, you may never really be the person who executes public speaking with finesse. It doesn't mean you can't and don't deserve the promotion. Ask your co-worker for a few tips and maybe watch them in action. Ask your other co-worker to give you a hand at tidying up your workspace. This will make them feel valuable and you can learn a lot from others who have different strengths.

You can impress your boss with your commitment to the job by being at work on time every day and turning in fabulous reports. Give your organizational skills a little attention but spend your time and energy on making your reports even better. That is your strength and that is what will get you promoted.

Chapter 7 - Health and Wellbeing

"To keep the body in good health is a duty... otherwise we shall not be able to keep our mind strong and clear."
~Buddha

It may seem impossible, but your self-esteem plays a role in your overall health and wellbeing. How you ask? When you don't feel good about yourself, you are less likely to treat your body with the respect and love it deserves. Earlier it was mentioned that one of the symptoms of low self-esteem was unhealthy addictions. Well, as you can imagine, an addiction to eating, drugs, alcohol or cigarettes is---unhealthy!

Now, this isn't to say that anybody who smokes, or drinks has a low opinion of themselves, but anybody who does it to excess does not respect their body enough to keep it healthy. It isn't as if we don't know about the risks of some of these dangerous habits. There are warning labels, billboards and commercials everywhere letting us know all these things are bad. Ignorance is not an excuse.

Some people who feel bad about themselves or have a rotten day at work or school will go home and binge on junk food. Obviously, this isn't healthy and may potentially lead to a number of health problems. The binge eater knows chips, soda and Ding Dongs are hurting their body, but they don't care enough about themselves to stop.

This can easily go the other way as well. One offhand comment about the way a pair of pants makes you look or a comment like, "Oh, maybe you shouldn't eat that 2nd helping," implying your weight is an issue, is like a kick to the gut. You immediately start analyzing every inch of your body and of course, you are going to find places that may have a few extra inches to pinch. This kind of unhealthy self-confidence level can lead to a dangerous eating disorder.

People don't always mean to be hurtful with flippant comments, but when somebody is struggling with a low self-esteem, those comments are painful and are taken to heart.

In fact, years of living with a low self-esteem can lead to depression. You have probably seen somebody with depression or maybe you have experienced depression. The person is often lethargic. They don't care about the way they look on the outside because on the inside, they feel horrible. Mental health is just as important as physical health. Depression is very serious and can lead to other health problems or even suicide if left unchecked. If are experiencing depression, please, see your health professional immediately.

Fortunately, there is hope for you and anyone who is letting a low self-esteem destroy their physical and mental health. You can build yourself up and take control of your life. As you start to feel better about yourself and realize you are worthy, you will automatically start taking better care of yourself.

Studies have proven that those who have a low opinion of themselves will suffer from certain health problems. Their life spans are also shortened. Some potential health problems include:

- Increased risk of high blood pressure
- Heart disease
- Stroke
- Cancer
- Stress

Fortunately, low self-confidence is completely curable! You can take back control of your life and reduce your risk of some of these health problems by taking steps today to boost the way you feel about yourself.

Establish Principles

Each of us needs to have our own moral code to live by. Yours will likely be a little different than your best friend's or your co-workers. It is your moral code and you have the freedom to decide what it will be. A moral code gives us parameters that help us feel as if we are on target, which is yet another way to increase our self-confidence.

Basically, your moral code will include established principles that govern how you live your life. When you uphold those principles, you feel good about yourself because you are living up to your own standards. You need to have some direction in your life. Without a purpose or direction, it is easy to get lost in the fray and feel alone and adrift. Many of us were brought up with some kind of religious beliefs or a set of rules our parents established. Those beliefs and rules will likely influence what your principles are today.

> *"I don't want to do anything that violates my own personal code of ethics and morals."*
> ~Michael Moore

This isn't something you really need to write down, but if it helps, go for it. You don't have to have a list of 20 things that you will and will not do. That may be too much pressure for you to live up to and if you fail to maintain your own high standards, you will only end up hurting yourself in the long run.

The following are just examples of some of the more common or standard principles that people like to set for themselves:

- Attend church regularly
- Abstain from alcohol
- Abstain from eating meat
- No cursing
- Be kind to others
- Respect others
- Be generous with your time
- Don't be judgmental
- Be honest
- Refuse to cheat to get ahead; Uphold high integrity

HEALTH AND WELLBEING

This is by no means a list you must follow. Your beliefs and expectations for how you live your life are completely up to you, so your list will be different and set according to your own code of ethics. When you uphold your beliefs, you will feel stronger in yourself. You are proud of your conviction to maintain your principles and will feel better about yourself in general.

A word of caution - do not set the bar so high it is unattainable. You cannot be perfect. You will have moments that you fail to keep to your principles. That is part of failure, but there is no need to bash yourself and countcract everything you have done to bolster your self-confidence. Accept that you made a mistake or slipped up and rejuvenate your efforts to maintain your principles in the future. This is a great time to take a step back and examine how you are living your life. Maybe you are in a relationship or surrounding yourself with people who do not have the same principles and are causing you to act in a way that goes against your moral code. This is where the hard work comes in. You must eliminate negative influences and those around you that don't have your best interest at heart. This is difficult, but definitely worth it in the long run. One final thought on this matter. It may be that the negative influence is a family member and you can't eliminate them from your life completely. This is understandable; however, you must set healthy boundaries and minimize your time with this person if you expect to rise above your low self-esteem.

Chapter 8 - 10+1 Quick Confidence Boosters

"We gain strength, and courage, and confidence by each experience in which we really stop to look fear in the face... we must do that which we think we cannot."
~Eleanor Roosevelt

You have come a long way in a short amount of time and, hopefully, you are already feeling a little better about yourself. You feel as if you really can get that promotion or you really can find a loving relationship that is healthy. All you needed was the confirmation you could. You can do whatever you set your mind to. Will you always succeed? Nope, but that isn't always a bad thing. Remember, failure is your friend and you are ready to make it work for you. Along with all of the stuff you learned throughout this book, you will likely want to have a few quick self-confidence booster tools in your knowledge bank. Sometimes you need something tangible to prove you are really taking steps towards enriching your self-confidence level. Positive affirmations are great, but some people need action.

These are some actionable things you can do to help enrich your life while increasing your overall self-esteem:

1 - Sign up for that class at the local college or community service office you have been thinking about for years. Pottery, painting, photography or writing classes are an excellent way for you to try out a new hobby. You may have a hidden talent that will blossom the second you give it a chance. A hobby is an excellent way to prove to yourself you are a multi-talented individual who isn't afraid to try new things. It will give you the chance to meet new people while exploring a world you were previously unfamiliar with.

2 - Buy a plane, train or bus ticket to somewhere you have always wanted to go. It doesn't have to be cross country. Jump in your car and head north or in whatever direction you wish. Give yourself the chance to break out of your safe zone and do a little exploring. It is exhilarating to try new things and with your new boost in self-confidence, you won't be afraid to leave the city you have been in for the majority of your life.

3 - Start writing in a journal. This is a therapeutic way to find out about your inner self and will help uncover some of those things that eroded your self-confidence. It will give you the opportunity to really discover who you are and why you deserve to be happy and confident. Through discovery, you will find healing. Through healing, you will find the courage and strength to keep going and you will restore your self-esteem.

4 - Buy a couple of posters with inspirational quotes and place them around your home. They are easy to find online via Google search. Sometimes we need to be reminded of our own worth and inspired to be great. If a poster or picture isn't your style, there are plenty of plaques that can be found. Place one on your desk at work or next to your bathroom sink. Try taping a card with a positive affirmation in the corner of your computer screen. You could use a Post-it® note and change the statement each week. Surround yourself with positivity and it will rub off on you. Make sure you change it up every couple of months. You don't want your inspiration to become mundane and just part of the wall or desk.

5 - Work on your posture to make yourself look and feel more confident. When you walk into a room, keep your head up and shoulders back. Walk with confidence and you will feel it. Make eye contact with others in the room. When you are nervous or feeling a little apprehensive, try this trick and feel the anxiety melt away.

6 - Try a new restaurant that serves exotic food. If you have never tried Indian cuisine, grab a pal and give it a try. Experience with a variety of cultures makes us feel more knowledgeable, which boosts our confidence. The next time you are in a social gathering, you will have something to talk about. Usually people who lack confidence are afraid to try new things, which can make them feel a bit like a social outcast. Get out and stretch your wings. Explore the world you live in!

7 - Save up to buy a power suit. When you look good, you feel good. You don't have to spend a lot of money. The goal is to find an outfit that makes you feel confident. Make it your lucky outfit and wear it when you have something really important to attend. It could be a job interview, a first date or even a family reunion. You deserve something spectacular. Be advised, however, this is not permission to go on a shopping spree that will put you in debt and kill the self-confidence you worked so hard to build up.

8 - Volunteer at a local soup kitchen, retirement home or some other charity in your neighborhood. When you are kind and generous to others, it makes you feel better about yourself. If you have the ability, try being a mentor to young adults who are

struggling. Check out your local Boys and Girls Club or YMCA to learn about different programs you can volunteer for. When we can give of ourselves, we feel valuable and important to the world we live in. We feel as if we have a vested interest in our community and it makes us feel as if we belong to something important.

9 - Join your local **Toastmasters** organization to improve your speaking and leadership skills. You'll meet new people and boost your confidence all within a no-pressure atmosphere. Your new-found communication abilities may just land you that promotion you've been shooting for.

10 - Set several small goals and achieve them. It could be something like cleaning out the hall closet or reading a book you have been putting off for a while. Maybe you want to get up a little earlier every day, so you can do yoga. Make it happen and you will quickly start to feel better about yourself. Goals are a major part of our lives, but they don't always have to be monumental or life-changing.

10+1 - Smile! When you smile, it is difficult to feel bad. Smile when you walk down the street. Smile when you walk into work. You will feel the smile and your self- confidence and mood will get a quick boost. Smiling doesn't hurt, and it is free. Your smile will be contagious. Imagine being in a workplace where everyone is smiling!

Conclusion

Thank you again for purchasing this book!

I hope the exercises and strategies you've learned are able to help you realize that you are worthy and capable of having a healthy self-confidence level. Everybody deserves to feel good about themselves and now you have the necessary tools get busy and start changing the way you feel about yourself. By immediately implementing these techniques you will gain back a healthy level of self-esteem and confidence, so you can achieve anything you desire!

The next step is to put what you have learned to work so you will start to see a positive transformation in your life.

Finally, if you enjoyed this book, please take the time to share your thoughts and post a review on Amazon. It'd be greatly appreciated!

Thank you and good luck!

References

http://www.counselingcenter.illinois.edu/self-help-brochures/self-awarenessself-care/self-confidence/

http://www.pickthebrain.com/blog/10-ways-to-instantly-build-self-confidence/

http://www.mindtools.com/selfconf.html

http://www.way2hope.org/overcoming_insecurities-nervousness.htm

http://www.lifeoptimizer.org/2011/04/23/failure-is-the-key-to-success/

http://unstuckcommunity.tumblr.com/post/63735769942/5-steps-to-make-failure-your-friend

http://thinksimplenow.com/happiness/20-ways-to-attack-shyness/

http://timemanagementninja.com/2012/07/10-reasons-why-confidence-leads-to-success/

[1]http://www.telegraph.co.uk/news/uknews/9474973/Key-to-career-success-is-confidence-not-talent.html

http://zenhabits.net/25-killer-actions-to-boost-your-self-confidence/

http://www.creators.com/health/david-lipschitz-lifelong-health/having-high-self-esteem-is-essential-to-good-health.html

5

Made in the USA
Lexington, KY
25 October 2018